Published by Creative Education
P.O. Box 227, Mankato, Minnesota 56002
Creative Education is an imprint of
The Creative Company
www.thecreativecompany.us

Design by The Design Lab
Production by Chelsey Luther
Art direction by Rita Marshall
Printed in the United States of America

Photographs by Alamy (Danita Delimont),
Dreamstime (Pebat, Scooperdigital, Webitect, Steve
Wilson), Getty Images (Sylvain Cordier, Fox Photos,
Cyril Ruoso/JH Editorial, Michele Westmorland),
iStockphoto (Rudy Suryana Sentosa, Renno
Sherman), National Geographic (TUI DE ROY/
MINDEN PICTURES), SuperStock (Minden Pictures)

Library of Congress Cataloging-in-Publication Data
Bodden, Valerie.
Komodo dragons / by Valerie Bodden.
p. cm. — (Amazing animals)
Summary: A basic exploration of the appearance,
behavior, and habitat of Komodo dragons, Earth's
heaviest lizards. Also included is a story from folklore
explaining why Indonesians respect Komodo dragons.
Includes bibliographical references and index.
ISBN 978-1-60818-087-5
1. Komodo dragon—Juvenile literature. I. Title.
QL666.L29B63 2013
597.95'968—dc23   2011050275

First Edition
9 8 7 6 5 4 3 2 1

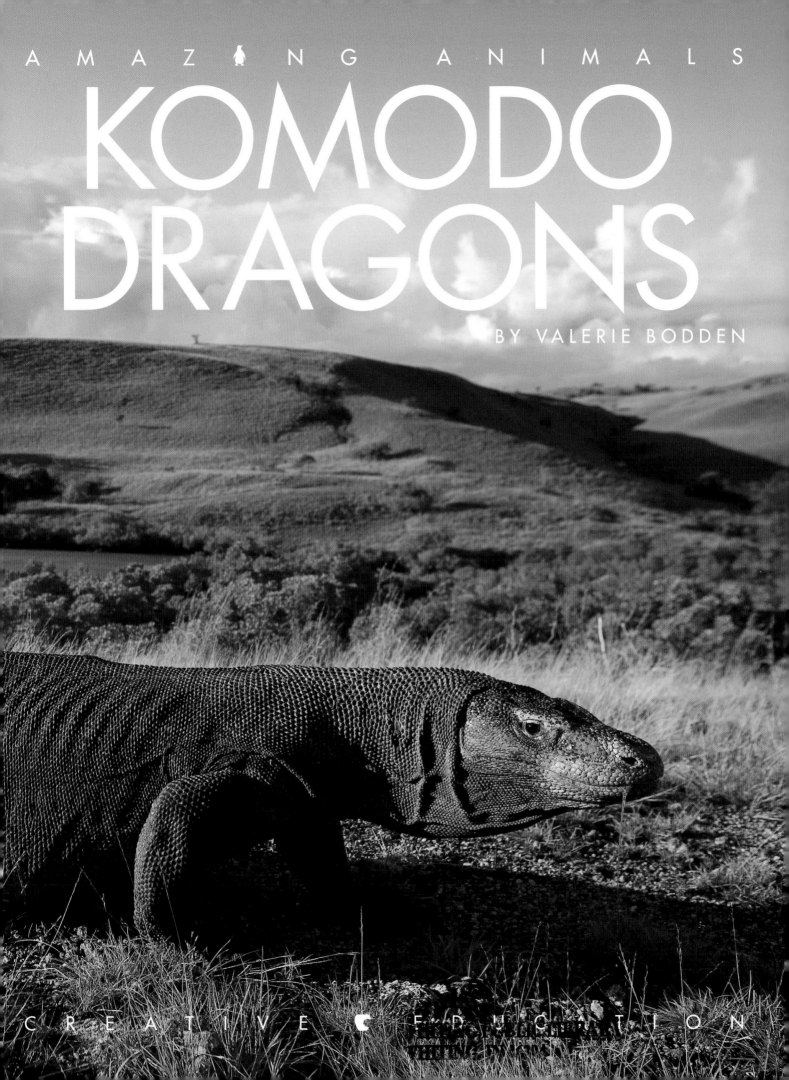

AMAZING ANIMALS

KOMODO DRAGONS

BY VALERIE BODDEN

CREATIVE EDUCATION

Komodo dragons belong to a group of lizards called monitors

Komodo dragons are the heaviest lizards in the world. Like all lizards, they are reptiles. Their bodies are covered with scales, and they are **cold-blooded**.

cold-blooded having bodies that are always as warm or as cold as the air around them

A dragon uses its tongue to "taste" the air around it

Komodo dragons have gray skin. They have sharp teeth and a **forked** tongue. When they bite an animal, they put **venom** into the animal's body. Komodo dragons have sharp claws and a long tail, too.

forked split into two or more parts

venom poison found in an animal's bite or sting

The biggest Komodo dragons are 10 feet (3 m) long. They weigh 300 pounds (136 kg). Komodo dragons can run 13 miles (21 km) per hour over a short space.

Dragons can move quickly, even though they are heavy

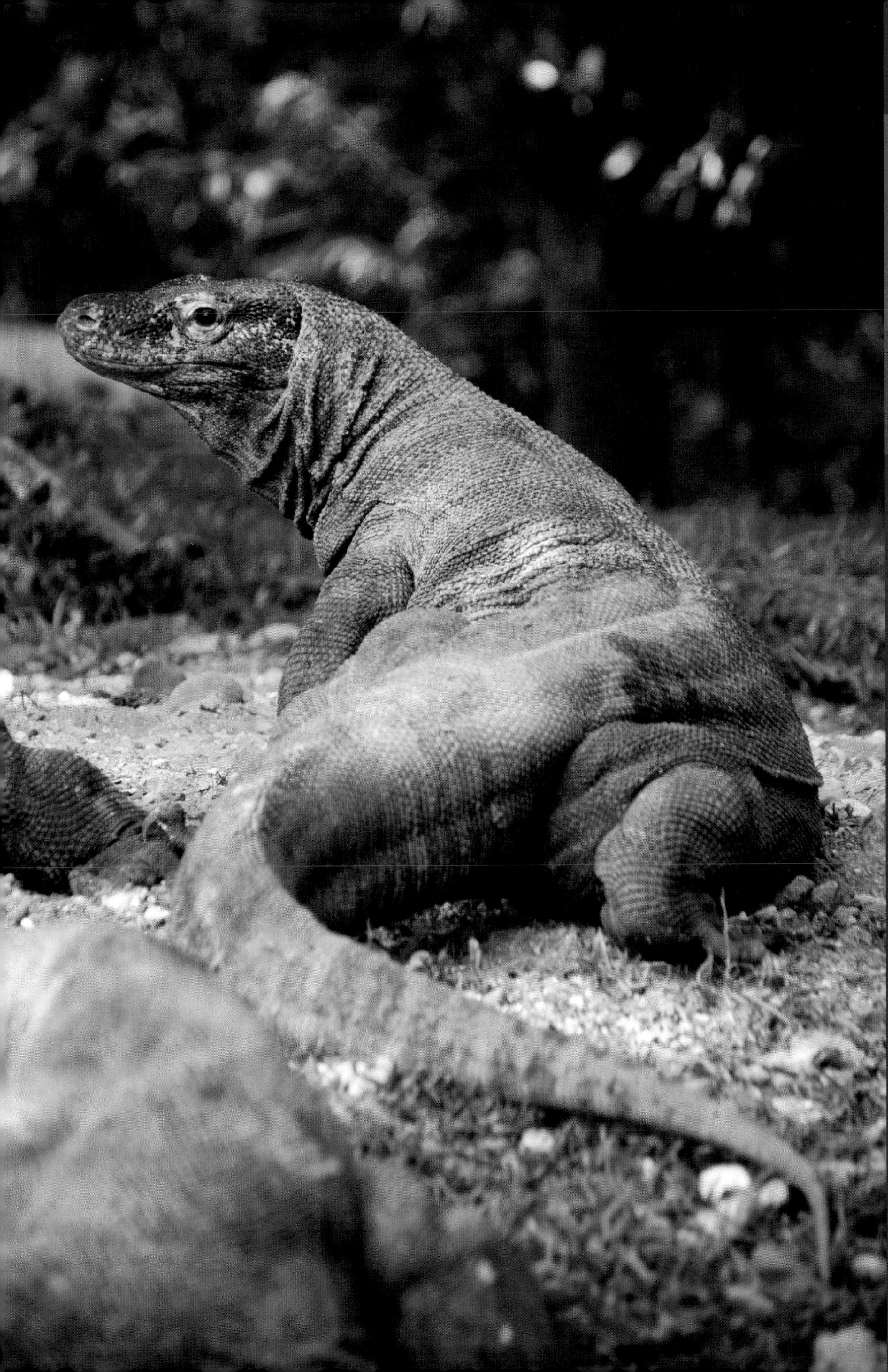

Komodo dragons can be found only on four or five islands in the world. These islands are part of a country called Indonesia. It is hot and dry on the islands.

People in Indonesia call Komodo dragons "oras"

Komodo dragons eat almost any meat. They search for dead, rotting animals. They also kill animals such as water buffalo and deer. Sometimes they eat smaller Komodo dragons!

A dragon can quickly swallow big chunks of meat

Baby dragons have more brightly colored skin than adults

A female Komodo dragon lays 10 to 30 eggs in a **burrow**. When the baby dragons come out of the eggs, they climb into trees nearby. There they can hide from birds, snakes, and other Komodo dragons. They live in the trees for four or five years. Adult Komodo dragons have no **predators**. They can live 50 years in the wild.

burrow a hole or tunnel in the ground

predators animals that kill and eat other animals

Komodo dragons spend most of their time resting. They lie in the sun in the cool morning and evening. They hide in burrows or in the shade when it is hot. After eating a big meal, dragons rest for up to a week.

Dragons may rest or stand guard near their burrows

Komodo dragons live alone. But sometimes a group of dragons gathers around a big meal. They often fight over the food!

A dragon's stomach gets bigger as it eats more food

Not many people live near Komodo dragons. But some people travel to see them in Indonesia. People have to be careful not to get too close. Otherwise the dragons might charge! Komodo dragons live in some zoos, too. It can be exciting to watch these powerful lizards move, eat, and fight!

A dragon may hiss to warn people that they are too close

A Komodo Dragon Story

Why do the people of Indonesia **respect** Komodo dragons? People there tell a story about this. Long ago, twins were born. One was a human boy. The other was a Komodo dragon girl. The twins did not know each other. But one day, they met. The boy gave his dragon sister a deer. Since then, people have shown respect for Komodo dragons.

respect to like or be pleased by something or to see it as important

Read More

Huggins-Cooper, Lynn. *Ravenous Reptiles*. North Mankato, Minn.: Smart Apple Media, 2006.

Owings, Lisa. *The Komodo Dragon*. Minneapolis: Bellwether Media, 2012.

Savery, Annabel. *Monsters*. Mankato, Minn.: Smart Apple Media, 2013.

Web Sites

National Geographic Kids Creature Features: Komodo Dragons
http://kids.nationalgeographic.com/kids/animals/creaturefeature/komodo-dragon/
This site has fun facts, pictures, and videos of Komodo dragons.

San Diego Zoo Kids: Komodo Dragon
http://kids.sandiegozoo.org/animals/reptiles/komodo-dragon
This site has Komodo dragon pictures and information.

Index